How to Start a Voiceover Career

(When You Have No Time or Money)

Kellian

Copyright © 2017 by Kellian

All rights reserved.

This book or any portion thereof may not be reproduced or used in any manner whatsoever without the express written permission of the publisher except for the use of brief quotations in a book review.

ISBN: 9781520523330

www.BestVoiceoverGirl.com

For those who invent the time to pursue the things they love.

CONTENTS

1	Background	Pg 1
2	My Story	Pg 3
3	Toolkit	Pg 7
4	Know Your Voice	Pg 16
5	Training	Pg 20
6	Demo	Pg 23
7	Finding Jobs	Pg 25
8	Website	Pg 39
9	Scams	Pg 44
10	Networking	Pg 54
11	Wrap-Up	Pg 57

1.
BACKGROUND

It's easy to start a voiceover career if you have thousands of dollars to throw at it and all the time in the world. Buy yourself a state of the art studio, pay someone to produce your demo, heck, go ahead and hire your very own fleet of airplanes that puts your website address on a banner and flies it over beaches. But, if you're like me when I first started out, chances are that you don't have ten-thousand dollars lying around, that you're not yet ready to toss away your current career, and that you don't have a spare 8-10 hours a day with which you currently do nothing.

What this book will teach you is everything I've learned through my voiceover career, which I started when I had very little time and only about $150 in the bank. This book is based solely on my experiences and what I've found to work. There might be better methods or people who have done it differently, but I have been fairly successful and am going to use this book to walk you through exactly what I did. By the end you'll know:

- Exactly what equipment I used and how much I paid for it

- Where and how to find jobs

- The exact phone scripts and emails I used to get higher paying jobs

- How to network without having to talk to hundreds of people

- When to invest more time and money in your career (later on and only on the important stuff)

- What resources I used to build my website, demo, and marketing materials

- How to avoid scams

2.
MY STORY

When I first started doing voiceovers six years ago, I was a poor college student. Scratch that, I was a poor college summer student. I was taking a physics class at Harvard Summer School (because I thought it would be easier than taking a lab class at my actual college... poor decisions all around). To my surprise and delight, I ended up making friends with (I kid you not) a foreign prince, an English Viscount, the heir to a Scottish restaurant chain, and few awesome folks from Texas. Unfortunately, I did not have even close to the means (a.k.a. cash) to keep up with their evening outings. I needed to find a way to make some extra money that wouldn't cost me anything up front, and wouldn't take up all of my time (because I wanted to spend THAT with the foreign prince).

I had recently seen an article in Reader's Digest

about a freelancing website where you could offer "a service for $5". I've always been a singer so I figured I'd "sing a song for $5". This, I quickly learned, was not as viable as I'd expected. Between having to record a backing track for each song, learn the tune, sing the song, and make a bunch of edits, many of the jobs took an hour or more. The freelancing website took a 20% cut, so I was making $4. If you do the math, $4 an hour isn't quite minimum wage... plus it was cutting into my time with friends. I explored the website to see what the other freelancers were doing and noticed the voiceover section. Voiceover was similar to singing... but, I quickly realized, the scripts were shorter, I didn't have to learn a tune, and I didn't have to record a backing track! I set up a profile, had a few orders come in, and the rest was history. To date, this has led me to voice characters in animated films, record for well know technical companies such as Mathworks, and even sing with Micky Dolenz (The Monkees) and Annie Golden (Orange is the New Black) on a musical that is going to be premiered on Broadway.

As you could see, my entry into voiceover was slightly more than dumb situational luck. Voiceover was something I wanted to try in order to make some spare cash on the side. Not something I wanted to seriously invest time or money in when I was first starting out. I would imagine that many readers of this book are in the same boat. How do you actually start a career in voiceover without fully investing yourself? After all, voiceover is an industry that, unfortunately, is rapidly becoming highly competitive and saturated. Add the fact that you don't have much (or any!) prior experience, time, or money to invest, and breaking might seem nearly impossible. Voiceover is a job that uses creativity, turns a good profit, and quite often, doesn't require you to leave your own home. Why wouldn't someone want to get into the business!

Because of this competition within the industry, there are hundreds of voiceover artists fighting for the same jobs. It's difficult to see how someone might be able to get started without going "full-force" (spending all their money and working 12 hours a day), things that those of us who want to 'just test the waters' cant afford. I wrote this book for those kinds of people. I want to share what I've learned through trial and error - that there **is** a way to do it without throwing away your current life.

Many of the books I've read about "getting started in voiceover" tout ways to "make millions with your voice!". I'm going to be honest and tell you that I find claims such as those to be a bit unrealistic. I can't guarantee that you're going to make a million dollars right from the get-go. What I can promise is that by the end of this book, you'll have a tested way of how to get started in the voiceover industry without sacrificing your current job and savings- because that's how I did it. This book will teach you how to get your feet off the ground in a way that doesn't require a full-time commitment or your retirement fund.

When I first started my voiceover career, I only had $150 to invest. I was able to take that $150 and turn it into a lucrative on-the-side voiceover business. I've since won and completed over 800 voiceover jobs in numerous industries, and it wasn't that hard! I am not a fulltime voiceover artist. I currently work 10-15 hours a day as an investment risk analyst for a large financial firm, yet I'm still able to do voiceovers. All it takes is putting in a few hours a week and consistently pushing. Everything comes down to persistence, marketing, and the right tool kit. The amount of money you make will directly correlate with the amount of time you put in. I've made the conscious decision to keep my voiceover career as part-time for now. Moral of the story: Your voiceover career will be whatever you make it, and you can shape it however you want.

3.
TOOLKIT

Before you can do anything related to voiceover work, you need the right toolkit so you can record and export voiceovers at a reasonable quality. This is where things are a little tricky. Since you're first starting out, you don't want to spend money on anything too fancy because, after all, you haven't made any money yet! You also don't want to use the built-in microphone on your computer or phone because you will get laughed at (trust me I've tried, and the sound is **NOT** passable. Unless phone and computer microphones get magically updated by the time you've read this book, DO NOT USE THEM!). Below, I've listed the bare minimum equipment you will need to record. I'll go through each piece and tell you what I used – both the cheap starter versions, and what I upgraded to once I started making money. The bare minimum list of equipment is:

1. Microphone
2. Recording software on your computer
3. Headphones
4. Your voice (well duh… you probably could have guessed this one)

All of these items could cost thousands of dollars (which you don't have). They also could be free or found at a dollar store (which isn't really worth it at all). I don't have all the market research on every single option, but here is what worked for me.

1. Microphone

The most important piece of equipment you will pay for is your microphone. Without a decent microphone, it doesn't matter if you have the voice of a god, because the end result will sound grainy and amateur. That being said, you also don't need to drop $20,000 on a high end, top-of-the-line, microphone. To be perfectly honest, for my first couple of years, I got away with using a Yeti Blue USB microphone that I bought for $150 from the apple store (they currently range from $130-$150 on Amazon, Google, the Apple store, etc., unless you can find a used one).

The Yeti Blue microphone is a basic USB microphone that plugs right into your computer (so easy!). This simplifies the recording process greatly.

This is especially useful if you're not a techie at heart and don't want to deal with anything too complicated. Not only is the set-up simple, but the Yeti is also a pretty decent microphone – not top of the line, but will definitely get the job done when you're still early in your career. I recorded 200+ jobs and auditions on the Yeti and never heard any complaints.

If some time goes by and you decide that you want to get more a professional microphone, then you can always upgrade to a non-USB microphone that connects to your computer via an audio interface. This will give you a better sound, and consequently, the option to audition for higher paying jobs. Plus, if you've already spent a few years with the Yeti Blue, you'll most likely have enough voiceover earnings to reimburse yourself the cost of the Yeti, and cover the cost of a new, nicer microphone. Personally, I didn't upgrade until I had made enough money to pay for all my equipment, new and old.

The microphone I upgraded to was to the Audio Technica AT2020 cardioid condenser microphone and I love it. It's a great step up from the Yeti Blue - a mid-tier priced microphone that's easy to use, produces a great sound, and one that I do not plan on replacing for a while. The microphone itself is actually cheaper than the Yeti Blue (currently goes for $84 on Amazon), but because it's not a USB microphone, you need to buy an audio interface with it. I use the Focusrite Scarlatti 2i2 (currently retails for $150). An audio interface is just a tool that allows you to connect an instrument, in this case a microphone, to your computer. In addition, since the Audio Technica microphone is freestanding, you'll need to purchase a microphone stand and potentially a pop filter. A pop filter is a netted guard that goes in front of the microphone to reduce unnecessary popping sounds from loud breaths and plosives (the sudden release of air into the microphone that happens after you speak certain consonants – ex. b, d, g, k, p and t)

I want to reiterate that I did not upgrade my microphone and accessory equipment until after I knew voiceover was something I was committed to and until after I had made a few thousand dollars from voiceover work; enough to cover the initial cost of the Yeti Blue and the new microphone/equipment I was purchasing. If you choose to go this route, you are letting your voiceover career invest in itself and don't have to spend as much of your savings up front. Again, this is just an idea of what I used, there are great resources online, and microphones are constantly getting better. A quick Google search of the "current best voiceover microphones" will definitely help you decide in case you want to explore other options!

2. Recording Software

The next basic piece of equipment you'll need to become a voiceover artist is recording software on your computer. This will allow you to record your voice and edit it (cut, splice, de-noise, etc.). If you have a Mac computer, you're actually already in pretty good shape. With a Mac, the easiest and cheapest option is to record through GarageBand – a program that comes pre-installed on your computer that is free to use. It has a very simple interface and comes pre-installed with a few settings that make your voice sound more professional. More often than not, I'll use their "natural voice" setting. It gives voiceovers the slightest touch of reverb (makes the voice sound a little fuller) without having to mess with any fancy settings. It also has a "de-noise" setting that can take out any unwanted backing noises the microphone may have picked up (you just have to be careful it doesn't take anything out that you wanted to keep in the recording!).

The one big downside to GarageBand is that it cannot export HQ (high quality) voiceover projects in .wav file format. It can only export in .mp3. The difference? Exporting a .wav file will produce a higher quality sound file that many professional jobs require, while an .mp3 file is a condensed sound file (the two might sound similar to the untrained ear, but any professional producer will be able to tell the difference). While many of the lower-paying jobs you take when starting out won't necessarily require .wav, it's good to have the option of either one. In my experience, nine times out of ten, an .mp3 file is just fine to send. That being said, as you go for more competitive jobs and your clients are in the higher-paying, more professional bracket, you'll most likely want to send .wav files. To note, I didn't have to export anything in .wav during my first year doing voiceover because I took less competitive introductory jobs, so I stuck to GarageBand and .mp3 (.wav however did become a requirement for my first "big" jobs down the line).

If you dislike GarageBand, don't own a Mac, or have a client that demands .wav, your other cheap "starting-out" option is to download Audacity – free audio editing software you can download onto your computer from online. I know many professional voiceover artists who use this software and love it. The plus about using Audacity is that it allows you to export your voiceover clips in .wav form, rather than just a basic .mp3. Audacity is also incredibly simple to use, so those who are "technically challenged" should have no problems at all. Note – on first download, Audacity does not actually even have the option to export in .mp3, but you can download an additional free software package to have it do so.

While GarageBand or Audacity should be more than enough, I updated my software a few years ago to Logic Pro X for $200. Logic offers more editing options and vocal effects than either GarageBand or Audacity, and is used for higher end studio production. I find it particularly useful since I sing in addition to doing voiceovers. That being said, it might not be worth the bang for the buck if you're happy with Audacity and are strictly doing voiceover work.

3. Headphones

My personal opinion is, when you're starting out, there's no need for fancy headphones. The point of investing in good quality headphones is that they allow you to hear the voiceover you recorded as clearly as possible, so you can pick up and correct any mistakes. I got by for years using the basic white apple headphones that came with my iPhone. I could hear just fine with them and there was no need for anything nicer. That being said, after a few years, and once I had the money for it, I upgraded to Sennheiser HD201 headphones because they fully cover my ears. This allows me to better hear my voice and the quality of the recording without any background noise. Very useful, but not necessary. I believe they were $15, so not super expensive either. Really expensive headphones are probably great, but I've never really seen the point.

When I record, I don't use headphones the entire time either – I like to listen to a final recording through my computer speakers. I've noticed that a good pair of headphones can actually make your voice sound fuller and honestly, better. So before I export any audio files for clients, I make sure to listen and edit my work both with and without headphones. This ensures that the sound quality is just as good either way because, guess what, your client is most likely listening to the recording you sent them on their crappy computer speakers, not hundred dollar headphones.

4. Your Voice

I probably don't need to explain why your voice is your most important piece of equipment. If you're going to be a voiceover artist, as simple as it may sound - don't get sick! If you get sick and lose your voice, it's game over. You can't work! And that's not good. Make sure you get your flu shot, wash your hands, and if you feel a cold coming on, get some rest. Everyone has a different opinion on this, but I swear by Zinc. If I feel any hint of a cold coming on, I start taking Zinc supplements immediately which generally either knocks the cold out or makes the duration of it much shorter. I'm not a doctor, and there are many people who disagree, but I'm convinced it works for me.

In addition to all this, one of the oldest, simplest tricks in the book is to just stay hydrated! If you're going to be speaking for hours, you don't want your vocal chords tired and dried out. And drinking right before you start won't necessarily work. When you drink, water doesn't immediately moisten your vocal chords. It generally takes about 2 hours for water to hit your vocal chords, so don't go into a recording session thinking that just bringing a water bottle will be good enough. You should start drinking water a good 2 hours before you start recording, if not just drinking consistently throughout the day!

In order to keep your voice in good health, it's also very important to warm up before you start recording. The best way to start is by doing lip trills- because it's nearly impossible to damage your voice in this way. So what is a 'lip trill'? If I tried to describe it in words I'd say, press your lips together and blow air out so you make a buzzing sound. Do this on a few notes, and then for some scales. However, if you've never seen or heard of lip trills before, just YouTube it really quick, because trying to explain it in words doesn't do it much justice. In addition to this, read through your script a few times. Take your voice up and down from it's lowest to it's highest on an "ahh" sound.

4.
KNOW YOUR VOICE

Once you have your toolkit in place, the next step is actually finding and getting jobs. In such a competitive environment, you have to be a little creative and a lot aggressive. In a polite way. The first step is to know where your voice fits in – what jobs are you most likely to get, and therefore, would be worth your time to pursue. Once you have that down, you can market yourself to specific audiences and in different ways via freelancing websites, your own personal website, and agencies (all of which will be discussed in the following chapters).

A lot of people tell me that they have "a good voice for voiceover", so they should have no problem breaking into the industry. I've always found this to be a little backwards. Yes – having the voice of Morgan Freeman is helpful, because that's where a lot of jobs are. What people don't realize though, is that those aren't the ONLY jobs out there. In fact, big movie trailer/documentarian jobs are probably NOT the jobs you'd even be able to audition for right out of the gate. The good thing? There are hundreds of jobs for every type of voice.

Think about the nerdy guy you hear on the radio advertising acne cream. The deep foreign body builder voice selling supplements. What about the stay-at-home mom telling you to buy children's toys? The baby voice on a children's iPhone app telling them to count "ten of the frogs"? Even the step-by-step instructions in a compliance tutorial at a financial firm needs to be voiced by someone. Guess what? The majority of voiceover jobs are for everyday voices. You don't have to be Morgan Freeman.

Because there are jobs for every type of voice, your first step towards marketing yourself as a voiceover artist is to identify the voice you have. Once you know this, you can appropriately market yourself and audition for the right jobs. Start paying more attention when you're watching TV or listening to the radio. Do you sound like certain people in certain commercials? What kind of commercials? What kind of people? Try to figure out where you fit in. If you have a deep commanding voice, it's probably not in your best interest to waste time auditioning to be the voice of a college student who is begging his teacher for higher grades. Know your age rage as well. Can you voice teenagers? Babies? Middle-aged adults? Grandparents? All of this information should be at your fingertips when choosing which jobs to audition for and telling potential clients what you can do.

It's also very important when you're first starting out to experiment and be open, don't put yourself in one box immediately. I have a younger, "girl-next-door", voice, so initially, I only auditioned for "young mom" and "college student" jobs. It wasn't until a year in, at a client's request, that I started attempting character and children's voices. (Character voice: think Mickey Mouse – a silly voice for a made up character). Turns out, I was pretty good at them, something I hadn't even considered! Now, at least 50% of my jobs are for children's voices, a voice I didn't even realize was at my disposal until I until I started experimenting with different ways to use my voice. It's important to stress that you're going to feel really silly when you start playing around with voices. They might not sound that good at first (or ever!), but this is the time to get out of your comfort zone and figure out what works. Plus, better to do it now instead of when you're in front of a client.

This is why you can't close off any avenues when you start. You need to figure out every type of voice you can do and then focus on those types of auditions. When I look for jobs I focus on those that call for "character voices", "girl-next-door", "young mother", "creepy child", "baby" etc. I would never audition for a job that called for a "body builder" or "middle aged golfer". Pick 4-5 phrases that would describe your voice and keep them in your arsenal. You should be consistently messaging your type of voice on your website, any freelancing profile pages you have, and whenever you contact a potential client. It also doesn't hurt to get the opinions of others. Ask your close friends, your mom, your coworkers, or anyone else you're close with, to categorize your voice and see if you get back similar or surprising responses.

5.
TRAINING

While natural talent and a cool sounding voice definitely play a part in being able to deliver effective voiceovers, there are some easy ways you can, and should, up your voiceover game. Something I did when I was a few years into producing my own voiceovers was to take a voiceover class at a local casting agency. Not only did this class give me different techniques in how to dissect a script and use my voice in a technically correct way, it also gave me a lot of great contacts. I still stay in touch with many of my classmates, and my teacher is the person who ended up producing my professional voiceover demos. It also doesn't hurt to take classes through a casting agency, so you start to get to know the different casting directors and learn about agency opportunities.

In a voiceover class, you can expect a teacher to

help you with script interpretation, diction, different types of voices, and to tell you any specific strengths and weaknesses of your voice. Often times, as part of a voiceover class, a teacher will actually bring students to a real recording studio and give them the chance to read scripts. If you're a beginner and have never been in a recording studio, this can be a huge benefit, as you don't want your first experience in a recording studio to be with a high paying client. It can also be a shock to hear what your voice sounds like coming from a high-end speaker rather then from inside your own head. Better to get this out of the way sooner rather then later.

The one negative side of voiceover classes is that they can be very costly. If you're just starting out and don't have the money, there are many online options that cost less or are free. Edge Studio is a great one. While they offer paid classes, they promote free online webinars and Q&A sessions that are very helpful. There are also books available for purchase that go into great depth on specific voiceover topics, such as script dissection or vocal warm-ups.

The greatest voiceover training tip I've ever received was when I was trying to learn new voices – children's voices, British accents, southern accents, characters, etc, the advice was… "just listen really really really closely". At the time, I thought this was an easy-way-out response from someone who just didn't feel like teaching me how they got so good at imitating other people's voices.

If someone asks you to do an Australian accent, don't say 'no' right away just because you've never tried it. Instead, go on to YouTube. Search for people speaking in an Australian accent of your gender, close to your own age, having a conversation. Watch the same 10-20 seconds of that video over and over again, and really listen to the pauses, pronunciation, tonality, and diction of each person. Then, watch those 10-20 seconds AGAIN and start speaking the conversation along with the people in the video. Do this until you start sounding like them. Sounds simple. Sounds crazy. But it totally works. This is how I learned children's voices, character voices, and a southern accent.

6.
DEMO

Possibly the most crucial thing you'll need in order to book voiceover jobs, is a professional-sounding demo. A demo is a relatively short audio clip showcasing your best work and your range of voices. This is generally the only thing potential clients will listen to when they decide whether or not to hire you. This is why your demo has to be AWESOME. If you're just starting out, the best you can do is search for some sample commercial scripts online that fit your vocal style. Record yourself reading all sorts of these sample scripts, then listen through and pick the few that you sound best on.

Adding a touch of background music can also make your demo sound a bit more professional. There are plenty of websites that offer this kind of backing music - just search online for "royalty free" music. When deciding between which scripts to read, what backing music to use, and how to splice everything together, it also helps to listen to professional demos, to get a feel for how they should sound. You can listen to mine at http://www.bestvoiceovergirl.com/demos.html, but I suggest you listen to a wider range then just that. Go to Voice123.com and search for "talent". This will pull up thousands of other voiceover artists, and their demos. You'll quickly be able to tell the difference between a good demo… and a bad one.

Personally, when starting out, I produced my own demo which was enough to get me work on smaller jobs and freelancing websites. Once I had saved up enough voiceover revenue, however, I paid $300 to have a professional demo produced. This is what allowed me to audition for higher paying jobs. Once you have the money, it's worth it. Not only can you hear the difference between a professionally produced demo and an amateur one, but having a producer as another set of ears to tell you which of your takes is best is incredibly helpful. Any recording studio in your area can do this, or if you're interested, I also now offer demo production services starting at $100 – feel free to contact me at kelliancross@gmail.com if you'd like details.

7.
FINDING JOBS

Even if you have all the right equipment, the perfect voice, and a professional demo, none of it matters if you can't get actual voiceover work. But where do you find jobs when you're first starting out? You don't have enough experience yet to attract a good agent (or any agent really), and probably don't have enough money to throw at the "pay-to-play" websites (we'll discuss this later). What I've found is that there are three main avenues to find voiceover work when you're looking for your first job: small local companies, talent rosters, and freelancing websites.

I can't stress enough that, when you're starting out, you're not just a voiceover artist – you're a manager and a marketer. There are hundreds of people fighting for every voiceover job, so in order to get a job, you have to be both creative and aggressive (politely!!). The more proactive you are about job hunting, the more work you'll get. It does take time, but if you stay tenacious and market yourself a little every day, eventually you will get work to some degree, and that "some degree of work" will turn into better opportunities as you build out your client base.

1. Small Local Companies

The first kinds of voiceover jobs I targeted were from small local companies – anything from restaurants, to private law firms and start-up gaming companies. While these kinds of companies won't be currently looking for a voiceover artist, it's up to you to tell them why they need voiceover work, and how you can help them. Working directly with smaller firms has added benefits as well, because as they grow, your work with them will also grow. If they get really big, then that's great for you since you were there from the beginning.

Create a list for yourself of possible companies you could contact. You can find them on Google, or just by walking around your town/city center. I keep all of my company contacts in an Excel spreadsheet. I list the company name, website, phone number and address at first. Once I've made a contact, I add additional information, such as who the contact person was and what their level of interest in me was. If they seemed interested, I make a note to follow up. If not, I know to not contact them again in the immediate future.

When you are ready to reach out to a company, there are two main avenues: cold calls or email. I suggest cold calls if you can, as it's much easier to get work once you have someone directly on the other end of the phone. What you'll want to do with this introductory call is introduce yourself and offer your services. What you'll start to realize is that most small businesses DO need voiceover work, even if THEY don't know they need it yet. You can offer to be the voice of their answering machine. You can be the voice of a new YouTube tutorial they're running for a product. You can be the voice of their local radio ad. There are thousands of ways to fit yourself in, you just have to get creative. To make it a little easier, I posted the phone script I use when cold calling, so you can have an idea of how to get the conversation moving:

> Hi, my name is *(your name)* and I'm a local voice over artist from *(your town/city)*. I see your company focuses on *(whatever their company does)* and I'm calling because I can help with recordings for answering machines, video tutorials or commercials. I just came out with a new demo package - is there someone I could send my information and demo to?

Since this is just the most basic of phone call

scripts, feel free to elaborate! Get them talking about what they and their company do. This information will give you a better sense of how you might fit it. No matter what, you want to leave the phone call with a name and contact information and follow up immediately! While cold calls might seem awkward and unnatural at first, they're by far the quickest way to get real, recurring clients, who will pay much more then ones on freelancing websites. There is really no downside to this method – the worst thing that can happen is that the person on the other end of the phone says "no" (and usually they're too polite to directly dismiss you anyway). It's not like you'll ever see them in person! I challenge you to do this 5 times in a row one afternoon with different companies. I promise, by the 5th time, it will feel like second nature. There is a famous line in sales training – "if a top salesperson tells you that they like cold calling people – they are lying." Don't feel bad about not liking cold calling – nobody does.

The other way you can market yourself to small local companies is through e-mail because, as I alluded to earlier, not all of us have time to make phone calls during normal business hours. The response rate is lower, BUT you can mass send e-mails much more quickly then you can make phone calls. I've even had weeks where I'll hire a remote assistant to send out e-mails for me. I give them access to my business e-mail (be careful with this, you don't want to be giving out e-mail access, passwords, or anything confidential to someone you don't know or trust), and then direct them to webpages full of start-up companies that might be interested in hiring me. I'll then have them spend a few hours e-mailing the heads of these start-ups, offering services on my behalf. Communication via e-mail gives you the flexibility to send e-mails on nights and weekends, making it more convenient for those of us who work a 12 hour day job! I've pasted the general template I email below.

Hello *[their name if you have it]*,

My name is *[your name]*, and I'm a *[your city]*-based voiceover artist. I do a lot of work with *[your city]*-based companies *[or something else that relates you to their company]*, voicing training videos, ads, and phone systems. I've just updated my voiceover demo package and was hoping to offer my services to *[Name of company]*.

I've attached my demos to this email, and you can also find them on my website: *[your website or demo information]*. I'm always glad to send free custom sample demos as well, so please let me know.

Thank you for your time,

Best,

[your name]

Side note about this e-mail template – I always attach my demos directly to the e-mail AND send a working link to a webpage with my demos. You want to make it as EASY as possible for a potential client to hear you.

If and when you get any kind of response, you should keep all the contact information from the responder in a contact sheet. Like I mentioned before, I use excel and keep track of the name, email address, phone address, company, and any personal notes I might have for each responder. This is useful for follow-ups and for sending out newsletters/emails when you're looking for more work.

When keeping all this contact information becomes tedious, I always remind myself of the "Paretto Principal" – that 20% of your customers will represent 80% of your sales. You need to keep track of your repeat customers, because they'll make up the biggest chunk of your work, and you need to make sure you stay in contact with them. The easiest way to retain your customers and keep them happy? Common sense. Respond to all emails within 24 hours, and be polite and friendly! You are not only a voiceover artist, but a business manager and customer service person.

2. Agencies and Talent Rosters

The next place to look for voiceover jobs is through talent agents and voiceover rosters. It is through these agents/rosters that you'll get access to more professional jobs and auditions with much larger payouts. A quick Google search for voiceover talent agencies and talent rosters in your area will pull up a pretty comprehensive list. From there, the best you can do is go on each agency's respective website, figure out how to submit yourself for representation (mail only, email, phone etc.) and then submit your application. After that, all you have to do is wait and see if they'll take you on.

Getting a talent agent is difficult, especially when you don't have any prior experience. Even if you get a talent agent, chances are you most likely won't be getting a lot of your work through him or her right away. However, any jobs that you DO get through your talent agency will more often than not pay a lot more than any work you get through personally contacting smaller companies and freelancing websites. Having a few non-exclusive agents (agents that allow you to work with more then 1 agent) in the background, marketing you while you market yourself is very helpful, and when agency jobs do come around, always make it a priority to audition for them! I didn't get an agent until I had been in the industry for three years. Just as a point of reference, over the last three years my agent has procured me 3 jobs and about 5-7 auditions. It is not crucial to have an agent, but once you're at a certain level, it does give you better access to higher paying and higher profile jobs.

3. Freelancing Websites

I have acquired the most clients and jobs from freelancing websites. A freelancing website is a website where you can post a profile page advertising your skills, jobs you'll do, and how much you want to get paid. Customers can then place an order from you directly through the website. The freelancing website takes a cut of this profit. Many freelancing websites also allow clients to post jobs that you can sort through and audition for. Freelancing websites are one of the best places to look if you're just starting out since there is no up front cost. The jobs are smaller and pay a lot less, so you can almost think about it as being 'paid to practice'. The good thing is, you'll get credits to put on your resume, get used to recording with your studio set-up, and make a little money on the side. Some good freelancing websites to check out are fiverr.com, upwork.com, freelancer.com and voicebunny.com (among hundreds of others). The website I started on was Fiverr.com.

The premise of Fiverr is that you will do

something for $5 (which they call a "gig"). This has since expanded to where you can sell multiple "gigs" and earn more than $5 a job. On Fiverr, you create a profile page for each "gig" you offer, where you explain what job you'll complete, how much it will cost, and how long it will take. For example, my voiceover gig states that I'll complete any appropriate voiceover, up to 100 words, in 1 day, for $5. On top of this, I offer extra services where customers can order multiple gigs for a higher word count or a faster turnaround time. You can see the concept on my fiverr page, located here: https://www.fiverr.com/krizcross.

There are some definite pros to using Fiverr. First, I have found that Fiverr takes less up-front work to get jobs compared to other sites such as upwork.com. Since Fiverr is gig-based, the customers find you, rather then you sorting through multiple jobs, spending time creating and submitting auditions, and then not getting 9 out of the 10 jobs you auditioned for. Another pro is that Fiverr is completely free to join, since they make money by taking a percentage of earnings you make. Currently, they take 1$ from each 5$ gig you sell (so 20%). While I have had luck with upwork.com, the jobs were very few and far between. That being said, you can make much more money per job on upwork then you could on Fiverr, you just have to put in a bit more work auditioning up front.

A newer website to the voiceover market with a slightly different business model is voicebunny.com. The idea is that a client submits a script they need read, and the first three (or however many the client requests) voiceover artists who want to audition, get to audition. And that's it. You get paid to submit these auditions, and then if the client accepts your read, you get paid the full amount. You have to be on your toes and incredibly fast to pick up the jobs. The competition is fierce. Whenever an audition comes in, you generally have less then 2 minutes to accept it, otherwise the job will close and go to a different voiceover artist. It's great for beginners as long as you have time to jump whenever an audition comes through, plus it can pay a little more then Fiverr.com!

4. Pay-To-Play Websites

In addition to freelancing websites, there are also "pay-to-play" websites, such as voice123.com and voices.com. "Pay-to-play" means you pay a high annual up-front fee that gives you the right to audition for jobs on the website. While they don't make commissions on each job you get, websites like these can be costly, especially if you're not yet established or high-end enough to compete with professional studios. The good thing about pay-to-play sites is that they offer more lucrative jobs from big-name companies. If you're going to spend the

$400+ to get access to these better auditions, your studio and demos better be good to go so you actually get jobs and the annual fee doesn't go to waste. This means you have to have a solid track record, a few jobs under your belt that you can put on your resume, a working studio set up with decent equipment (because they **will** ask you what you use), and a KILLER demo.

I signed up with voice123.com between 2013 – 2014, and I learned all this the hard way. My studio was meh (this was before I had upgraded my equipment), my demo was just okay, and I only got 1 job the entire year because of it (huge waste of money). You should only sign up with these pay-to-play websites if you are in a position to compete with professional studios. In addition, even if you have the demo and the studio, jobs on these websites are still highly competitive. Expect to be auditioning and following up on potential projects every day, because you'll be competing against full-time voiceover artists that can turn projects around in 24 hours.

Below I've listed some of the freelancing and pay-to-play websites I've tried personally or researched along with their pros and cons. Again, I suggest starting with fiverr.com and voicebunny.com and working your way up.

Website	Skill Level	Pros	Cons
Fiverr	Beginner	No auditions, Free to sign up	Pay a 20% commission on all jobs, Cheaper jobs
Voicebunny	Beginner	Paid to practice, Lots of jobs	Have to be super speedy to jump on auditions
Freelancer	Medium	Free to sign up, Higher paying jobs	Competitive, Have to audition for each job
Upwork	Medium	Free to sign up, Higher paying jobs	Competitive, Have to audition for each job
Voices (Pay to Play)	Advanced	Most lucrative jobs, Brand name jobs	High up front investment, Heavy competition
Voice123 (Pay to Play)	Advanced	Most lucrative jobs, Brand name jobs	High up front investment, Heavy competition

4. Social Media

By far one of the easiest places to market yourself is on social media. Advertise your voiceover skills on Facebook, YouTube, Twitter, or even Instagram. You will be amazed at how many of your friends work for companies or know people that need voiceovers. You'll also be amazed at how many of your friends are completely willing to help you. Spread the word and explain how your voiceovers would be perfect for phone messaging systems, product demo videos, radio advertisements, etc. Let your network know what you do and how it can help them, then let them help you.

I can't stress enough though, that it's on YOU to explain what you do. Most people won't realize what voiceovers can be used for. Many of my friends didn't even know it was a job. Just remember that every company has a phone system. Most companies need general marketing. A few companies need dubbed videos. There are hundreds of different capacities in which you could provide voiceover work. I was just in touch with a friend who worked with a highly conservative, private, financial firm… why would they ever need voiceover work? Turns out that each of their employees has to go through compliance training, which featured an animated video implementing (you guessed it) a voiceover artist!!! This just proves that voiceover really can fit in at any company, you just need to figure out why that company needs a voiceover and then explain it to them.

Don't forget when "bothering" friends on social media, that your skills are actually quite valuable. Having a professional, unique voiceover can help companies bring in and keep customers. It can make a huge difference, especially at start-ups, since having a professionally recorded answering system, or tutorial video will make the company look more established and professional.

8.
WEBSITE

Beyond social media, you need a website. This is a must, not at first, but once you're looking to expand your business. Your website will serve as a landing place that links everything together – your pictures, services, reviews, demos, EVERYTHING. For those of you with less-than-acceptable technology skills, such as me, this might seem like a daunting task. However, with a little bit of time (a.k.a. a lazy Sunday morning), it is easy and doable to set up your own website.

The way I did it was to purchase a domain name and hosting through the website "JustHost.com". I personally like JustHost.com because it auto-renews my domain name (so someone doesn't buy it out from under me) and provides simple drag-and-drop options for website deign. That being said, there are a ton of other great hosting sites out there that do the same exact things (my other favorite is squarespace.com), this just happens to the be the one I picked.

JustHost gave me the option to use different web designing tools. I ended up using Weebly (the other popular option would be WordPress), because it seemed the simplest. It's a drag and drop format where you can simply, and quickly, lay out your website. It took me maybe 2-3 hours to get something up and running (you can see it at: bestvoiceovergirl.com). Registering for a domain name and purchasing a basic hosting package cost me about $160 all in. So again, I suggest you start with a freelancing site and work your way up to having your own website once you've made some money.

In terms of website design, there are a few things you should absolutely have on your website. At the very least, you'll need to post your demo and your contact information, so people can decide if they like your voice, and then reach out to you if they want to work with you. In addition to your demo and contact information, it doesn't hurt to have a few pictures of yourself. This will legitimize you and help the client see you as a real person with business potential. Please realize that I'm not talking about a blue-steel high-fashion model shot. Your look should match your voice.

Most voiceover work is in advertising and promotion, and most companies will want a happy, friendly, personable voice advertising their product. Unless you are trying to play the voice of Scar in the "Lion King", you should probably look friendly and inviting in your picture. You should look like someone people will WANT to work with. Below are two different picture's I've tried profiling on my website, so let's play the "guess which picture got me more voiceover jobs" game:

Hopefully you guessed the picture on the left! It's much more approachable, friendly, and happy! This photo projects that I'm a professional and friendly person who would be more than happy to work with any potential client.

If you have the time and resources, you want to let the client get to know you through your website. The more they see you as a real person, the more likely they will be to want to work with you. You can do this by having a biography page, client testimonials, a video introduction, and, if you want to get extra fancy, a direct purchase option and a logo. I had my logo designed on fiverr.com for $25, and I'm really happy with it! Proof that there are definitely cheap ways to get professional looking designs:

bestvoiceovergirl.com
The best choice. The best voice.

Another thing to think about when designing your website is branding. Once you've identified what type of voice you have, figure out what your message is, and reflect that on every page of your website. For me, I'm the friendly, young voice used for marketing and phone messages, so I wanted to present myself in a clean, friendly and simple way. You better believe I don't market myself as a 50 year-old business mogul. I know that my voice is perfect for ads featuring young mothers or children, so I keep my website cheerful.

This is absolutely not necessary, but I even went as far as to give my voiceover career and website a color: purple! My website is purple and white. My logo is purple, and my demo play buttons are purple. I also chose to highlight any words relating to "voiceover" in purple. Little things like this can help you stand out, you just have to pick your "thing". I was also incredibly careful to keep all colors, fonts, and text sizes consistent. I'm a believer that clean simple websites get the most notice, so I've kept mine basic, no fancy background or flashing colors. The focus is on my demos, and that's it. I also want to note that, in addition to voiceover, I also model and sing. Because I wanted to keep my messaging consistent, I don't feature singing and modeling prominently on my website. My website focuses on voiceover, while the singing and modeling offers are buried on an "other services" tab.

9.
SCAMS

If you're going to be in the voiceover industry and doing a lot of work via e-mail, you have to be very careful, because there are a lot of people who want to take advantage of the fact that they'll never meet you face to face. I want to discuss some of the voiceover scams out there and how to avoid them. The rule to live by is that money should never, ever, **EVER** leave your hands (as I will show through the example below). You are providing a service, so the person hiring you should be in charge of the studio fees, booking fees, agent fees, or any other kinds of fees you could think of. I had the unpleasant experience of dealing with a scammer last year. I've posted the exact e-mails below so you could get a sense of what you might be dealing with. The person in question, I've changed his/her name to "Pete" had posted an advertisement for voiceover work that I had said I was interested in and asked to see the script:

---

from: Pete
to: Kellian
subject: RE: Casting Call

Hi,

I received your email indicating your interest. I would not be able to send you the script because my client has copyrighted it and confidential is of utmost importance. Therefore the script shall be release a day before the project. I hope you understand?

As part of my working policy and ethics, I receive part payment from any client before I proceed with any job and balance you immediately after the job, this is to identify a serious client and ascertain the job. So I will get in touch with our client and part payment will be mailed to you, until you receive and confirm payment before the recording will hold. Your total pay for the job is going to be $850 as discussed. Part payment of $400 will be mailed to you first and you get the balance of $450 on the final day of the recording. I hope you understand?

Do Send me your payment details for issuing

a check as to which our client is to mail out your part payment to you in the details below:
Full name:
Complete Mailing address (No P.O Box):
Phone numbers (Cell and Home):

After you confirm the part payment which should serve as transportation and mobilization.
Get in touch with your required details as soon as you can. The date of the Recording shall be communicated to you once I get all the details. Concerning the date of the recording, you have the opportunity to choose the two most convenient days for the recording between 15th and 24thth of June and do indicate it in your next reply.

Regards,
Pete

----

from: Kellian
to: Pete
subject:Re: Casting Call Update

Hi Pete,

No worries about the script, completely

understand, payment method also makes sense.

In terms of dates, by far the best for me are nights and weekends and I would be available any night (5:00 on) and all weekend (the 18th and 19th)- if that's an option? If weekends and nights are not possible, the best dates for me would be the afternoons of the 16th and 17th (but I'm decently flexible since there's advanced notice).

Let me know, thanks,

Kellian

---

from: Pete
to: Kellian
subject: RE: Casting Call Update

Hi Kellian,

I will like to say congratulations to you on your new job. I want to assure you that everything would work out fine as planned. Kindly get back to me to reconfirm your interest in the job.

Venue: 380 Main St Medford, MA 02155
Date: 18th and 19th of June

Time: 5pm- 6pm

As said in my previous email, your initial payment would be made out to you. Payment will be sent out and awaiting confirmation of this from my client. Once you receive the payment, you are expected to cash and deposit it into your bank account. After which, you deduct your initial payment of $400 to guarantee your participation in this project, and then send the remaining balance to the consultant engineer who will take care of all technical aspect of the job and studio rental with other planning. Your remaining balance of $450 will be given to you on the final day of the recording. I hope this is clear?

As soon as i receive a confirmation from you, i would let you know when to receive the payment. I look forward to your email. Also do reconfirm the information below:

Full name for payment:
Full mailing address:
Phone number and best time to be reached:

Regards,
Pete.

----

from: Kellian <kelliancross@gmail.com>
to: Pete
subject:Re: Casting Call Update

Hi Pete,

That sounds great, still interested and I can make those dates and times at Rescue Productions. Do I need to do anything in terms of booking the studio time, or has all that been taken care of through the consultant engineer? I would not be able to submit any balance to the sound engineer, however, they'd have to be paid directly through you, otherwise I wouldn't be able to take the job. Let me know if this works, thanks,

Kellian

---

from: Pete
to: Kellian
subject:RE: Casting Call Update

Hi Kellian,
It is not as if the engineer can't be paid separately but she is on a transit handling some project at the moment. Sending payment separately will cause delay on this project because she won't be able to process

it and that is we thought of pairing her with you. Sorry for any inconvenience this must have caused you and i promise it won't happen in any future project.
Regards,
Pete

----

from: Kellian Cross
to: Pete
subject:Fwd: Casting Call Update

Gotcha - unfortunately I wouldn't be comfortable paying out of the check you send as a lot of scams like this have been taking place recently. If circumstances change and you can pay her directly let me know and I'd be happy to take the job.

Kellian

That was the last I heard from "Pete". I went online and searched his/her name, and he/she had apparently targeted many other voiceover artists as well. The way the scam works (if you haven't already figured it out!) was that "Pete" would send me a check worth double the amount I was getting paid. I would then need to pay a "consultant engineer" out of the money I was given. This is already a little fishy… if "Pete" could write a check for me directly, why couldn't he write a check for the engineer?

Had I gone through with this, I would have received and deposited the check. Often, banks don't detect bad checks immediately, so it could actually look (for a few days) like the money had successfully been deposited into my bank account. I would send off the money to the engineer, the engineer's check would clear, and the check "Pete" sent me would not – I would be out $400.

Scams are not always easy to spot, but often, some basic fact checking and Googling can be incredibly helpful. For instance, I drove by the studio "Pete" had booked for me, only to find out that it has been completely shut down for years, even though it was still coming up on a Google search. Always do your research, and, if its not possible to drive by the studio, call the studio directly to see if time has actually been booked before you show up.

Also note the poor spelling and bad grammar in the e-mails from Pete. Many times, emails you get from these scammers will be poorly worded, or use bad grammar and it's usually on purpose. Don't make the mistake of thinking that just because the scammer's e-mail is poorly worded that they live in a foreign country and speak another language. Many scammers will often use poor grammar to make you think that they're overseas, or just plain stupid, when usually, they're not. Also be aware that if you do fall for a scam, others are more likely to go after you, as you'll be pegged as an easy target. Always use your best judgment, be careful when giving out personal information, and remember that money should never **EVER** leave your hands.

If someone has tried something like this on you (whether they succeeded or not) it's very tempting to get angry and want take action, after all it seems very unfair, not to mention illegal. The online consensus on retaliating against attacks like these is DON'T. Actually getting back at a scammer might be harder then you think. It's easy to forget that for many of them, scamming people out of money via the internet is their full time job, and they're probably pretty good at it. This means they are most likely skilled coders and hackers who are better than you at both hiding and accessing information via the Internet.

I've read stories about people who tried to get back at scammers, only to end up on automated call lists, where they were getting scam calls so often they had to change their phone numbers. If anything, your best plan of action would be to file a complaint with your state's attorney general office so they're aware of the problem, takes about 5 minutes to do. You could also report him or her to the Federal Trade Commission (FTC) or Federal

Communications Commission (FCC).

10.
NETWORKING

Ah, networking. Some of us live for it, others would rather crawl under a rock and die. Unfortunately, if you're a "crawl under a rock and die" type person, you're going to have to suck it up and learn how to network (just a little!). I'm not a born networker or extrovert, but I've learned some tips and tricks that have helped. Just remember, good networking isn't necessarily about talking to as many people as possible. I don't consider "good" networking to be going to big industry events, talking to 50 people, and getting as many business cards as possible. While there's a chance that speed networking may give you a few new contacts, the number of contacts doesn't really matter, the number of **quality** contacts does. It's far better to have two really good contacts than 40 business cards. Not only that, but I've found a much better focus isn't the act of "networking" itself, but the act of "keeping up your network".

Again, having 40 business cards isn't going to do you a lot of good. However, keeping up connections with friends, and people you know and have already worked with in the industry will. One of the best contacts I have, I met through a voiceover class I was taking after work. Because of the class, we already had a good rapport and he later helped me record my voiceover demos. We stayed in touch through various events and he's become a great mentor and friend.

In order to have a "quality" contact, you want to be in touch with the person every once in a while, especially when you don't actually need something, because you don't want to be the person who only reaches out when they need a favor. When you make a potentially good contact, follow up – send an email or a thank you note. If it's been a few months, send them a quick e-mail with an article you think they'd be interested in, or ask a question or for their advice. Be warned though, asking pointless questions or sending irrelevant articles can hurt you and make you seem a little annoying. When you do these follow ups, make sure they're as relevant and meaningful as possible and timed appropriately.

Also, don't forget that your network doesn't just have to be industry experts and voiceover artists. Believe it or not, people like to help you (this is a concept that took me a really long time to accept) and family and friends will generally have your back. You never know whom a friend will know or how a family member might be able to help you unless you ask. For instance, my roommate's girlfriend, a girl who I had known for over a year, had a close friend working at Nickelodeon. A great contact for a voiceover artist like me that I hadn't known about because I hadn't bothered asking! I've known many fellow performers who've made connections though friends and family that resulted in them getting jobs in big-budget movies and video games. The point is, use the network you already have, and make an effort to keep up any new connections you make.

I know I've mentioned this many times before, but I want to stress how useful it is to keep a spreadsheet of all the contacts you've made who have helped you. And remember, you want to keep not only their names, addresses, and e-mail, but also any personal notes you have about them. How you met them, what they've done for you, what you've done for them, etc. Information like this comes in handy the next time you need to reach out.

11.
WRAP-UP

Guess what?! While having an agent is nice, when starting out, you need to be your own agent. And marketing fleet. And accountant. And talent. And web developer. And producer. And publicist. You basically need to be everything! The good thing is, it can be done, and it can all be done in your spare time. Even if all you give yourself is 15 minutes a day, you will still be ahead of the pack. Far ahead.

Personally, I was able to do it all on an average of about a hour and a half per week, give or take one or two days where I spent the afternoon working on my website or business model. When starting out, that's all you really need, and once you start getting more work, and making more money, you get to make the decision whether or not to transition into a full-time voiceover artist.

So... start now! Schedule out 15 minutes a day to dedicate to your new voiceover company and you will be doing way more than most. Plus you've already put a few dollars into buying this book, and I'd hate for that to go to waste. It would be better to use some of these tips and tricks to make the investment in this book pay off!!

I would also love to hear your success stories and am happy to answer any questions you might have. You can reach me at: kelliancross@gmail.com. Your voiceover career will be whatever you make it, so might as well make it great

ABOUT THE AUTHOR

Kellian was born and raised in the sunny suburbs of Massachusetts with an entrepreneur for a father and singer for a mother. She went to college in Pennsylvania and earned degrees in music, mathematics, and economics while completing outside courses in voiceover and modeling. While serving as a glorified paper shredder during an internship at MTV, she started her own voiceover and vocals company. Since then, she has completed over 800 voiceover projects - her favorite was voice-acting an 8-year old boy in an animated film premiered in Singapore. In order to not let her mathematics degree go to waste, she also worked at a large financial firm as an investment risk analyst. For fun, she like to go to barre for exercise, bars for non-exercise, and record as much as possible. Oh, and fun fact, she's worn miss-matched socks since the age of five.

Printed in Great Britain
by Amazon